Celebrations in My World

Holi

Lynn
Peppas

Crabtree Publishing Company
www.crabtreebooks.com

Crabtree Publishing Company

www.crabtreebooks.com

Author: Lynn Peppas
Coordinating editor: Chester Fisher
Series and project editor: Penny Dowdy
Editor: Adrianna Morganelli
Proofreader: Crystal Sikkens
Editorial director: Kathy Middleton
Production coordinator: Katherine Berti
Prepress technician: Katherine Berti
Project manager: Kumar Kunal (Q2AMEDIA)
Art direction: Dibakar Acharjee (Q2AMEDIA)
Cover design: Tarang Saggar (Q2AMEDIA)
Design: Neha Kaul (Q2AMEDIA)
Photo research: Farheen Aadil (Q2AMEDIA)

Photographs:
Alamy: Mike Abrahams: p. 20; ArkReligion.com: p. 21; Imagebroker: p. 4;
   The London Art Archive: p. 17; David Pearson: p. 5
Corbis: Martin Harvey: p. 6; Reuters: p. 28; Narendra Shrestha/epa: p. 9
Dreamstime: p. 10, 26; Jatin Chadha: p. 29; Nikhil Gangavane: p. 23
Fotolia: Nikki Zalewski: p. 7
Surinder Gulati: p. 13
Hindu Images: Akhilesh Kumar: p. 31
Indiapicture: Bhaswaran Bhattacharya: p. 14; Hemant Mehta: p. 22;
   Marryam Reshii: p. 11; Shalini Saran: p. 15
Krishna.com: p. 12
Photolibrary: Photos India: p. 19
Photoshot: Michelle Poire/World Picture New: p. 8; UPPA: p. 24
Pix and Design: p. 18, 27
Reuters: Ajay Verma: p. 1
Shutterstock: Kentoh: p. 30; Paul Prescott: p. 16
"Silsila" Image Courtesy and Copyright: Yash Raj Films Pvt. Ltd.: p. 25
Visage Images: front cover

Library and Archives Canada Cataloguing in Publication

Peppas, Lynn
   Holi / Lynn Peppas.

(Celebrations in my world)
Includes index.
ISBN 978-0-7787-4753-6 (bound).--ISBN 978-0-7787-4771-0 (pbk.)

   1. Holi (Hindu festival)--Juvenile literature. I. Title. II. Series:
Celebrations in my world

BL1239.82.H65P46 2010   j294.5'36   C2009-902024-6

Library of Congress Cataloging-in-Publication Data

Peppas, Lynn.
   Holi / Lynn Peppas.
      p. cm. -- (Celebrations in my world)
   Includes index.
   ISBN 978-0-7787-4771-0 (pbk. : alk. paper) -- ISBN 978-0-7787-4753-6
(reinforced library binding : alk. paper)
   1. Holi (Hindu festival)--Juvenile literature. I. Title. II. Series.

BL1239.82.H65P47 2009
294.5'36--dc22

                                    2009014151

Crabtree Publishing Company

www.crabtreebooks.com   1-800-387-7650

Published in Canada
Crabtree Publishing
616 Welland Ave.
St. Catharines, ON
L2M 5V6

Published in the United States
Crabtree Publishing
PMB16A
350 Fifth Ave., Suite 3308
New York, NY 10118

Published in the United Kingdom
Crabtree Publishing
White Cross Mills
High Town, Lancaster
LA1 4XS

Published in Australia
Crabtree Publishing
386 Mt. Alexander Rd.
Ascot Vale (Melbourne)
VIC 3032

Contents

A Hindu Festival

Holi is a **Hindu** festival. Hindus celebrate Holi on the day after the full moon in February or March. During the festival, Hindus celebrate the beginning of spring and **honor** important events in Hindu **mythology**.

People of all ages celebrate Holi.

DID YOU KNOW?

People used to celebrate Holi for five days. Today, most people celebrate Holi for two or three days.

Holi is a time for merrymaking.

People have been celebrating Holi since ancient times. It is one of the least religious Hindu holidays. It is a time for Hindus to let go and have fun.

5

What is Hinduism?

Hinduism is a religion. It is the world's third most popular religion. Many people in India are Hindu. Hindus believe that there is more than one god. They believe there are many gods. They pray every day.

In Hinduism, the **soul** is **eternal**, which means it lasts forever. Hindus believe that it is wrong to kill or harm any living thing. Hindus believe that when they die, their soul is reborn in a different body.

Hindus worship in places called temples.

"Om" is a special **symbol** used in many prayers. It is used to represent Hinduism.

DID YOU KNOW?

Hindus say "Om" at the beginning and end of many prayers.

7

Around the World

People throughout India celebrate Holi. People in the United States, Canada, Bali, Guyana, Trinidad, Nepal, the United Kingdom, and other countries also participate in this fun and colorful festival.

People in Queens, New York celebrate Holi.

DID YOU KNOW?

Holi is sometimes called Holaka or Phagwa. Some people also call it the Festival of Colors.

Holi is a week-long celebration in Nepal. On the first day a bamboo pole called *chir* is placed in the street with strips of cloth attached to it. The cloth represents good luck charms. The throwing of colors takes place on the last day. Afterward, *chir* is taken to a bonfire.

People in Nepal put *chir* in place on the first day of Holi.

9

Celebrating Spring

During Holi, people celebrate the end of winter and the beginning of spring. Holi began as an **agricultural** festival, marking the colors and liveliness of spring. People celebrated the harvest of the winter crops.

In India, spring is a colorful time.

DID YOU KNOW?

*During spring in India, fields are green and lush. The color green is a sign of **prosperity**.*

Many fruits and vegetables grow during spring.

Holi is a time to celebrate the richness of the land. People celebrate in different ways depending on which countries or regions they are from.

11

Good and Evil

Prahlad was devoted to the god Vishnu.

According to one Hindu legend, the Holi festival comes from the story of Holika and her nephew, Prahlad. Prahlad represents "good," and Holika represents "evil" because she tried to kill him.

DID YOU KNOW?

For many people, Holi is a celebration of "good" over "evil" because Prahlad survived Holika's attempt to kill him.

Holika was burned in a blazing fire, and Prahlad was saved.

Prahlad's father wanted Prahlad to worship him instead of the god Vishnu. Prahlad refused. Prahlad's angry father decided to have him killed. So, Prahlad's aunt, Holika, who could not be hurt by flames, carried him into a fire. But, in the end, she died, and Prahlad was saved.

13

Lord Krishna

For some people, Holi honors the Hindu god Krishna, who lived 5,000 years ago. According to legend, Krishna asked his mother why his girlfriend Radha's skin was so light and his skin was so dark.

Krishna sometimes played the flute for Radha.

DID YOU KNOW?

Holi is also a celebration of the love between Radha and Krishna. Images of Krishna often show Radha standing beside him.

Krishna liked playing tricks on Radha.

Krishna's mother told Krishna to put color on Radha's face and see how her skin changed. Radha got even by rubbing paint on Krishna. Since then, people celebrate Holi by throwing colored powder or water on one another.

Lord Shiva

Another myth connected to Holi tells the story of the Hindu god named Shiva. He has a third eye that flashes fire. The goddess Parvati wanted Lord Shiva's attention. Parvati asked Kamadeva, the god of love, for help.

Shiva is often shown with snakes around his neck.

DID YOU KNOW?

Lord Shiva is known as the god of destruction. He represents darkness.

The day celebrated as Holi is the day Kamadeva was brought back to life.

Kamadeva shot an arrow of love at Lord Shiva so he would notice Parvati. Shiva became angry, and burned Kamadeva to ashes. Holi honors the day Shiva agreed to bring Kamadeva back to life.

17

Forgetting Differences

During Holi, people have fun. It is a time to relax with family and renew friendships with people. All people—men and women, rich and poor, young and old—forget their differences and come together.

Holi is a time to have fun with people you would not normally celebrate with.

DID YOU KNOW?

Singing and dancing are also important parts of the Holi celebration.

Men and women like to play tricks on each other just like Krishna and Radha.

In some parts of India, there are contests between men and women during Holi. One tradition is for men and women to take part in pretend battles. The men are not allowed to fight back, however.

Burning of Holika

On the evening of the first night of Holi, people light huge bonfires. Lighting these bonfires is a Holi tradition. It reminds people of the story of Holika and Prahlad, which represents good overcoming evil.

This Holi bonfire is at the City Palace in Udaipur, India.

DID YOU KNOW?

Some people believe that ashes from Holi bonfires bring good luck.

Some people throw offerings to the gods into the flames of the bonfires. In some parts of India, people burn **effigies** of Holika. An effigy is a small figure that is meant to represent something or someone that is disliked.

Some children act out the story of Holika and Prahlad during Holi.

Colors

Throwing colored powder and water is another Holi tradition. People throw and smear the powder on one another until they are completely covered in different colors. Red, green, yellow, blue, and pink powders are common.

People throw colored powders for Holi.

DID YOU KNOW?

Krishna liked playing tricks on his friends. Throwing colors helps people remember Krishna's tricks.

This woman is selling Holi supplies.

People usually wear their oldest clothes during Holi. They use plastic bottles, balloons, water pistols, bicycle pumps, and other objects that squirt. They spray people with as many colors as they can.

23

Holi Music

Music and songs are another important part of the Holi festival. Some people play Holi music for one month before the festival begins. Holi music includes traditional folk songs and songs from movies.

● Children in London, England, play drums for the Prince of Wales and the Duchess of Cornwall during a Holi celebration.

DID YOU KNOW?

The dohl is a type of drum. It is made from a wooden shell with goat skin on either end. A person plays it with two sticks.

This picture is from the movie *Silsila*.

There are many popular Holi songs from **Bollywood**. Bollywood is a nickname for the film industry in India. Bollywood films are often musicals. The Holi songs from Bollywood make people dance and have fun.

25

Delicious Foods

Many people prepare and eat special foods during Holi. These foods include dried fruit, chocolates, and other sweets. People also eat *mathri*, which are similar to salted crackers. People drink *thandi*, which is a cold drink made with milk, sugar, seeds, and herbs.

• Dried fruit is a favorite snack during Holi.

DID YOU KNOW?

Many Indian foods contain a spice called turmeric. Turmeric gives food a bright yellow color.

People enjoy crispy *pakoras*.

In northern India, many people enjoy crispy, golden *pakoras* at Holi celebrations. *Pakoras* are vegetables, such as onions, peppers, zucchini, and eggplant, fried in a **batter**. Cumin, coriander, and turmeric are some of the spices in the batter.

27

Playing Holi

There are many ways to celebrate Holi! In Rajasthan, India, Holi is combined with the Elephant Festival. Elephants are painted in bright colors. Tourists have a chance to play Holi while riding on the backs of the elephants.

These people are having fun playing Holi while riding on elephants!

DID YOU KNOW?

During Holi, people often say "Bura na mano, Holi hai," which means "Don't feel offended, it's Holi!"

Join in on a Holi celebration this year.
Visit www.colorsofindia.com/holi/paste.htm
Color an image of yourself, your friends,
your family, or your pets for Holi.

People let loose and
have fun during Holi.

Holi Quiz

Take this quiz to find out how much you know about Holi.

1. When is Holi?
2. Who celebrates Holi?
3. Who is Krishna?
4. Which Hindu god has a third eye?
5. What is the phrase people often say to one another during Holi?

Some temples are brightly decorated with statues of Hindu gods.

DID YOU KNOW?

There are nearly one billion Hindus in the world. There are many Hindu temples and centers in the United States and Canada.

People wish one another Happy Holi.

Answers:

1. People celebrate Holi in February or March.
2. Hindus celebrate Holi.
3. Krishna is a Hindu god.
4. Shiva has a third eye.
5. People often say "Bura na mano, Holi hai," during Holi.

Glossary

agricultural Relating to agriculture or growing crops for food

batter A thin mixture of flour and liquid

Bollywood A nickname for the film industry in India

effigy A small figure that represents something or someone that is disliked

eternal Lasting forever

Hindu A follower of the Hindu religion

honor To show respect or admiration for something or someone

island An area of land surrounded by water

mythology A collection of stories about gods and goddesses

prosperity The state of being successful

soul A person's spirit

symbol Something that stands for something else

Index

Printed in China—CT